More Hot Stuff to Help Kids Chill Out: The Anger and Stress Management Book

Jerry Wilde, Ph.D.

Illustrations by Kara M. Webb

LGR Publishing
3219 N.W. C St.
Richmond, IN 47374

LGR Publishing
3219 N. W. C St.
Richmond, IN 47374

More Hot Stuff to Help Kids Chill Out

Illustrations by Kara M. Webb
Cover Design by Polly Wilde

For information: LGR Publishing
(800) 369 - 5611

Printing History
First Printing 2000

ISBN : 0 - 9657610 - 3 - 7

PRINTED IN THE UNITED STATES OF AMERICA
10 9 8 7 6 5 4 3 2 1

Acknowledgments

There are a lot of people to thank for helping me with this book. Let's start with our kids. Anna typed the last word of this book so it could be said this project would never have been completed without her. A special thank you goes to our son, Jack, for comic relief and general insanity. You're awesome, dude!

The people who deserve most of the credit for this book are the people who have written, called, and emailed to tell me how much they enjoyed the first book. Your enthusiasm about the original *Hot Stuff* inspired me to write this version.

A big thank you goes to Kara M. Webb for the great illustrations.

Finally, to my wife and best friend, Polly, thanks for the cool looking cover and for being a great partner on this journey.

This book is dedicated to Rory Gallagher and his music.

Jerry Wilde

My thanks goes out to Jerry Wilde for the opportunity to be part of this book. I would also like to thank my family.

A heart felt thanks goes to my parents for all of the love and support they have given me. Thanks to Matt, Tasha, and Leah for their love and support and the many wonderful childhood memories. For rejuvenating my youth and my outlook on life, I thank my very special nieces.

Finally and most of all, thanks to my husband and kindred spirit, David, whom I love dearly for his strength and support.

Kara M. Webb

Other books by Jerry Wilde

Hot Stuff to Help Kids Chill Out: The Anger Management Book

Teaching Children Patience Without Losing Yours (with Polly Wilde)

An Educator's Guide to Difficult Parents

Why Kids Struggle in School: A Guide to Overcoming Underachievement

Treating Anger, Anxiety, and Depression in Children and Adolescents: A Cognitive-Behavioral Perspective

Anger Management in Schools: Alternatives to Student Violence

Rational Counseling with School-Aged Populations: A Practical Guide

Surviving and Thriving as a Blended Family

Rising Above: A Guide to Overcoming Obstacles and Finding Happiness

The Subject is Joy: A Path to Lifetime Contentment Through Value-Based Living (with John Wilde)

Praise for *Hot Stuff to Help Kids Chill Out: The Anger Management Book*

"I am excited about using Dr. Wilde's Hot Stuff as a therapeutic tool when working with adolescents who have anger issues. My clients respond with enthusiasm to its humorous, relevant, and matter of fact approach. I especially like using the Anger Survey at the beginning and end of treatment as a way to measure the changes in their thinking."

Dr. Lisa Wiens
Neighborhood Counseling Center
Wadena, Minnesota

"Your book, Hot Stuff, really peaked the interest of my tenth grade class. Two students who have serious anger management issues actually asked to look at the book and wanted me to order them copies. I am excited by the prospect of students wanting to work on their issues and I am thrilled I may have found the book to allow them to do just that!!"

Charlene Belletsky
Communities in Schools
Allentown, Pennsylvania

A Short Note to the Adults

Here we go again! Let me once again thank all the counselors, teachers, and parents who encouraged me to write another book on this topic. It's nice to know the original *Hot Stuff to Help Kids Chill Out* was valuable in your work with children and adolescents. I hope this new edition can live up to your expectations.

What you're going to find in *More Hot Stuff* is an expanded version of the original. I tried to review the most important features of the first book, expand in areas where it was needed, and add new information to make this book more complete. For example, there is more information on stress management in this edition. Students rarely possess an intuitive understanding of the connection between stress and anger. They don't understand that during periods of high stress, it is easy for them to lose their cool. So helping kids learn to manage stress is an important component to any good anger management curriculum.

As I stated in the original *Hot Stuff*, when I read a book by a so called "expert" I can't help thinking, "I wonder how long it's been since this person has actually counseled a kid or facilitated a group." For what it's worth, I'd like you to know I've run numerous anger management groups and counseled thousands of kids so these lessons are field tested. I've written three books on anger management prior to this work (The original Hot Stuff to Help Kids Chill Out - LGR Publishing, Anger Management in Schools: Alternatives to Student Violence - Technomic Publishing, and Treating Anger, Anxiety, and Depression in Children and Adolescents: A Cognitive-Behavioral Perspective - Taylor & Francis). I hope you find this book a useful addition to your professional library.

If you have any questions or comments, I'd enjoy hearing from you. Feel free to call me at (765) 939 - 8924. There is one exception. I really don't want to hear from readers who have a burning desire to point out a missing comma. There are probably a couple of other grammatical errors...deal with them the best you can. Everyone else is encouraged to call. (Hey, I'm just trying to be honest.)

Best of luck and keep up the important work that you do!

J.W.
November 2000

Introduction

Now that you're finally sitting down to read this book it's probably a sign that:

1) You read the first one and laughed at all the stupid Elvis Presley jokes. Somehow along the way you also managed to get a better handle on your anger, but there's still some room for improvement.

2) You didn't read the first one. You still think Elvis is alive and living in Montana. You're reading this book because you can't think of a single thing to do to get out of it!

3) You **are** Elvis and you've developed an anger problem because this guy keeps writing anger management books and using you as the punch line for all his stupid jokes. Also, you're sick of Montana and want to return to Graceland.

Okay, I absolutely promise that is the last time I'll use Elvis in this book. I just couldn't resist one more.

4) You've decided to *really* work on your problems with anger.

I hope the answer is # 4 but either way, keep

reading because learning to manage your anger is an important skill.

These are angry times we're living through. Everybody gets angry some of the time and that's okay. Anger is a normal human emotion and there's nothing fundamentally wrong with anger. *It's what we do with anger that's important.* Anger can move us in both positive and/or negative directions. Always keep in mind that *anger is okay, violence is not.*

These are also very stressful times to be alive. Just like anger, stress is not evil. In fact, the only folks without stress are dead people! The key is to learn to manage your stress rather than having your stress manage you.

Before we get going, I thought you might like to know a little about me and why I wrote this book.

Name:	Jerry Wilde
Lives In:	Indiana, but don't worry you Cheeseheads. I still love Wisconsin. You can take the boy out of the cheese, but you can't take the cheese out of the boy.

Hair:	Got plenty
Wife:	One (named Polly)
Daughter:	One (Anna)
Son:	One (Jack)
Cats:	Three (Spazmo, Herb, and Mosh)
Favorite Musical Artists:	Rory Gallagher (please check him out, you'll be glad you did), AC/DC, Led Zeppelin, Korn (Are you READY!?!?)
Hobbies:	Listening to music, running, playing guitar, reading books, refusing to be too serious, pretending to be an adult, sports
Cool Things:	Health, music, my family, Green Bay Packers, Iowa Hawkeyes, sunny days, Diet Mt. Dew, guitars
Uncool Things:	Ignorance, wasting time, violence, committees

I decided to write this book because I believe I can help you learn the skills necessary to control your anger and stress. I've written a lot of other books (yes, I know I need to get a life), but those books were for teachers and counselors. This one is just for you, not for adults.

Over the years I've worked with hundreds of kids and had a lot of luck with the things I'm going to try to teach you. You can learn to have a less stressful life, but it won't be easy. You can have a life that isn't filled with anger related problems, but that choice is up to you. If you work hard at the things in this book, your angry episodes will decrease. If you don't work hard, you'll still have the same difficulties you've been having with anger and stress. **You are free to choose.** Keep in mind you are also free to experience all the unhappiness your heart can bear. I can't, and won't, stop you. But I'm pretty sure I can help if you want it bad enough.

Learning to manage your anger and stress is like learning any new skill. It takes a lot of hard work and practice. There are absolutely no short cuts, but the rewards are worth the effort. Let's move ahead now as you don't have any time to waste. Your anger and stress have probably been slowing, but steadily, hurting your body for quite a few years already. It's time to get to work.

Before we get too far into this, let's take a closer look at the kinds of attitudes you have. Complete the anger survey below as honestly as you can. There are no wrong answers. Circle the number which best reflects how strongly you agree or disagree with each statement.

The Anger Survey

Strongly Disagree — Strongly Agree

1. I get angry when things don't go as planned.

   1 2 3 4 5 6

2. Other people make me angry.

   1 2 3 4 5 6

3. Life should be fair.

   1 2 3 4 5 6

4. When I don't do well, I get very angry with myself.

   1 2 3 4 5 6

Strongly Disagree					Strongly Agree

5. Things have to be my way or I get angry.

   1 2 3 4 5 6

6. The world has to be a better place to live.

   1 2 3 4 5 6

7. My family can <u>make</u> me get angry.

   1 2 3 4 5 6

8. There are a lot of things that ought to be better than they are right now.

   1 2 3 4 5 6

9. I can't control my temper.

   1 2 3 4 5 6

10. I get mad when people don't act like I think they should.

    1 2 3 4 5 6

TOTAL__________

Anger is O.K., Aggression is NOT

There's something important that needs to be covered in this book. I'm going to spend a lot of time telling you what's wrong with anger, but you also need to know that anger--when it's under control--can lead to positive outcomes. Nothing is ALL bad, right?

What's Good About Anger?

Like I've said before, anger is not necessarily bad...it's what we do with it that is important. Anger can lead to a lot of problems, but it can also be helpful in certain situations.

1. Anger can tell us something.

Anger often let's us know when our personal values are being violated. In that way, anger tells us what we believe in and that's very important. For example, if you become very angry when someone lies, that's a sign that honesty is important to you. If your anger flares when someone is late, that's telling you that being on time is important.

Below I want you to write down three things you have been angry about. Next, try to identify which of your personal values were violated, which is what caused you to make yourself angry. Use the two examples from above (dishonestly and being late) as a guide.

"Things I Get Angry About"

1.____

____

2.____

____

3.____

____

Now see if you can figure out which of your personal values were violated prior to the anger incident.

1.____

____

2.____

____

3.____

____

2. Anger can warn you of the potential for violence.

Anger is often associated with aggression, however anger is never the **cause** of violence. **Aggression is a choice.** If you have a tendency to become violent when angry it's important to realize your anger may be trying to tell you something.

Think of anger operating like a warning siren. When you feel the anger coming, acknowledge the fact that you may become aggressive. Then it's important to be smart so you don't hurt someone, hurt yourself, or get into serious trouble.

Later in this book there will be a lot of ideas to keep yourself from exploding. Pay particular attention to the technique described in the section on **Distraction**.

3. Anger can energize you.

Anger is included in our range of emotions for a reason. It is an emotion that often signals the body, "Hey, wake up, we might need to do something here! This could be dangerous."

The body then release chemicals into the blood stream to get ready in case there is need for a physical reaction of some kind. These chemicals make us more alert, ready to run or fight, and generally more capable of handling whatever is about to happen. And that's a good thing.

4. Anger can encourage you to stand up for your beliefs.

As was explained, anger is usually a sign that your personal values have been violated. For example, if you see a bully picking on a smaller student, you may become upset about the situation. Your anger might motivate you to get involved because you think it's wrong to act like a bully.

If you didn't dislike bullies, you wouldn't get involved. However, when bullies picking on kids goes against your personal beliefs, you might say or do something. That's great. We all benefit when we help each other out.

Most people never realize that the word "motion" is contained in the word "emotion." That's not a coincidence either. Feelings often put us "into motion" and that's one of the reasons we have emotions.

So anger is beneficial at times. See if you have some ideas of other ways in which anger can be helpful. Write them down below.

1.____

____

2.____

____

3.____

____

What's the Deal with Anger?

Like I said earlier, anger is a normal human emotion and each of us is entitled to *all* of our feelings...the good ones and the not-so-fun ones.

Anger can motivate you to stand up for yourself or right a wrong, but it can also cause you a lot of unnecessary difficulties. That's especially true of instances when anger turns to rage. I like to think of rage as "temporary insanity" because it allows us to do all kinds of crazy stuff.

One of my goals with this book is to help you learn to have control of yourself. An important first step toward that goal is to examine your anger. Place an "x" next to each statement that is true for you.

When you get angry do you...

Physical

☐ Grind your teeth?

☐ Feel your face getting red?

☐ Get a funny feeling in your stomach?

☐ Feel tense all over?

☐ Start sweating?

Behavioral

☐ Cry?

☐ Destroy things?

☐ Get violent, hit, push, shove, etc.?

☐ Walk away but then simmer for hours?

☐ Yell and scream?

Thinking?

☐ Think of revenge?

☐ Can't stop thinking about the person or event?

☐ Can't concentrate on school?

Emotional

☐ Feel "up tight" or anxious?

☐ Feel like hurting someone?

☐ Become depressed?

☐ Feel energized?

☐ Fear that you might lose control?

On the next page draw a picture of what your anger looks like.

"My Anger"

Before we go much further, I want to spend a little time on some important ideas that will increase your likelihood of learning to cope with stress and anger. Here's the part of the book where I try to take away all the excuses you'll use NOT to improve. But before I do that I've got to make certain you understand a few basic ideas about thoughts, feelings, and the connection between the two.

Self-Talk

People talk to themselves all the time. Most of the time we are not aware that we are even doing it. It's sort of like breathing. We breath all day, but never think of it (although you're noticing your breathing right now, aren't you?)

Sometimes we tell ourselves things that are true and usually those ideas help us get along in life. Other times we tell ourselves incredibly stupid things that do nothing but mess up our lives.

Some students I work with like to think of the ideas we tell ourselves as "CDs or tapes." When your CD is playing a good song in your head, you're usually happy and doing fine. When your player is pumping nonsense into your mind, guess how you feel? B-A-D.

Now here are some examples of untrue things you may tell yourself about your anger. Place an "x" next to each statement you agree with.

- ☐ "When I'm mad, I *have to* let it out."
- ☐ "Holding in my anger is bad for me. It's better for me to let it out."
- ☐ "The person I'm mad at is a total loser and deserves to suffer."
- ☐ "Other people or things make me angry."

If you believe these thoughts, it will be very difficult for you to learn to manage your anger. All of these thoughts are false, but a lot of people believe them. Don't feel bad if you agree with some or all of them. **Those thoughts are the reason for your problems with anger.** Now it's my job to try to convince you these ideas are wrong. Here goes...

1. "When I'm mad, I *have to* let it out."

Some students believe that when they become upset they *have to* express their anger or let it out. Not true. If somebody offered you $17.5 million dollars **not** to vent your anger, do you think you could remain calm? I think you could and I've got 17.5 million reasons why!

So letting it out is a **choice** you make. Nobody ever **has** to let it out. You're not a balloon and you won't pop.

2. "Holding in my anger is bad for me. It's better for me to let it out."

It's amazing that almost everyone I know believes this and it's not true. There's a ton of evidence that letting out your anger is, in fact, bad for you. Your body is harmed by either holding it in or letting it out, but more damage in done when you vent your anger. Plus, when you vent your anger you may feel better for a short time, but you're actually increasing the likelihood that you'll become angry in similar situations in the future.

3. "The person I'm mad at is a total loser and deserves to suffer."

First off, no one is a *total* loser and no one

deserves to suffer. Everyone has both positive and negative qualities to them. Simply because you don't like someone doesn't mean that person deserves to suffer.

4. "Other people or things make me angry."

This is one of most commonly held, and damaging, beliefs that keeps people from learning to manage their anger. This is false!

Think of it this way...there is no such thing as an "emotional transplant." We can give people a heart or kidney,but each of us creates our own feelings. That's why people feel differently about things.

You still don't believe me, do you? Let me give you an example and see if that will make more sense.

If 100 students got a grade of "B" on an exam, would they all feel the same way? Of course not, some would be happy, some would be sad, and others might not even care how they did. If events *caused* feelings, how could the same event cause different feelings? It couldn't because people create feelings by the ways in which they think about the event.

Here's a picture of a student who received a "B." Draw on his face how YOU would feel with that grade. Write down the feeling you would have next to your drawing. Now look at other students' drawings. Did everyone feel the same way? Yes No

If you answered "no" then the grade didn't cause your feeling. Your *thoughts* about the grade did!

This is so important that I'm going to make certain you've "got it" before we move on. **You, and only you, control how you feel**. So what makes you angry?

Y - O - U

I can hear some of you still saying, "Dr. Wilde has definitely gone off the deep end. He doesn't have both oars in the water. The lights are on but nobody's home. He's crazy if he thinks I make myself angry."

Okay, here's another example that might help you wrap your brain around this idea. Let me tell you a story to help you understand the point I'm trying to make.

Let's pretend you were walking down the hall and somebody knocked all of your books out of your hands. How would you feel? You'd start whistling a tune just because you were happy to be alive, right? No, seriously, you'd probably be angry, right?

When you turn around to see who hit your books you realize it was a blind student who accidentally bumped into you. Now how would you feel? Still angry? Probably not.

Here's the important part. You still got your books knocked out of your hands so **things happening** (such as the "atomic book drop") can't make you angry. So it must be something else.

That "something else" is your THOUGHTS. Your thoughts, beliefs, and ideas are what make you angry...not your parents or teachers or friends. Let's take a closer look at the example of getting your books knocked out of your hands.

What would you probably be thinking just as your books went flying?

____

____

Could it be something like, "You stupid moron. Watch where you're going"? Those thoughts would definitely make anybody angry.

But what would you think to yourself when you saw it was a blind student?

____

____

Maybe something like, "He didn't mean to do it. It was an accident." Those thoughts would calm you down.

Notice how the event (getting your books scattered) stayed the same but the feelings changed as your thoughts changed. That's because **your thoughts influence (and largely control) your feelings**.

This is good news! If other people and things made us angry, what would be the point of trying to learn to handle our anger? There wouldn't be a point because YOU would have no control...other people would be controlling you like a puppet.

Now that we've answered the million dollar question, we have our work cut out for us. Now we need to learn how to start hearing our thoughts before we get angry. Not easy, but not impossible.

Unlike the girl in this picture, YOU are not a puppet. You are in control! You choose how you react! There are NO strings attached to you!

Anger Causing Beliefs

Do you remember the answer to the "really important" question?

What is it that causes you to be angry?

Write it down here.

____

If you put down "My thoughts cause me to be angry," give yourself a pat on the back and tell everyone, "If I was any smarter, I'd be two people." A lot of adults don't realize they make themselves angry and most of your teachers probably don't know it either.

Here's something fun to do. Walk up to your mom, dad, teacher or principal and say, "I was wondering if you knew that my misbehavior does not actually *cause* you to become angry. Your anger is something you create. I have no control over the thoughts that bring about your anger." Then RUN!

If I was any smarter, I'd be two people.

No, I'm kidding. Then smile and say, "I've been reading a fascinating book. I'll let you borrow it when I'm finished." If you do that, you'll be "da man." Even girls who do this will be "da man."

But what exact type of thoughts make you angry? Let's find out.

Look at this list of thoughts and put an "X" after the ones that probably cause anger.

1. "People shouldn't be such idiots."______
2. "I don't like math but I guess I can stand it."_____
3. "Even though my parents can be hard to live with, they're not the worst parents in the world."_____
4. "If people don't listen to what I say, they deserve to suffer."_____
5. "My life stinks because people don't do what I tell them to do."_____
6. "This class shouldn't be so boring."_____
7. "I wish my parents would let me go out this weekend but if they don't, I'll still be able to have some fun."_____

If you put an "X" next to # 1, 4, 5, and 6 give

Look at this dude. You can practically SEE him getting smarter!

yourself another pat on the back and say out loud, "I've got brains I haven't even used yet." Those four statements will probably bring about anger because they all do one thing:

THEY DEMAND SOMETHING

The other statements are still "hoping" something different happens but they're just hoping, not demanding. You've all heard the old saying, "Where there's smoke, there's fire." Here is a new way to use that saying.

"Where there's an unmet demand, there's anger."

Take a minute and think of a time when you got angry and try to remember what you were demanding. For example, when you got mad for a getting a detention you didn't think you deserved, you were probably demanding two things:

1) That you not get the detention and

2) That you be treated fairly by your teacher.

Does that make sense?

Take an anger example from your life and see if

you can figure out what you were demanding and write it down here.

____

____

If you're having a hard time, here are some hints. Look for the "hot" words that bring about anger. They are words like the ones listed below:

Should
Shouldn't
Must
Must Not
Have to
Ought to

Can you hear yourself thinking any of those "hot" words? Any words that are demands may bring about anger.

Some of you may be thinking, "Okay Dr. Wilde dude, what do YOU think when somebody does something you don't like or you have some really bad luck? Don't you get angry?"

Hey, I get upset just like anybody when someone treats me unfairly or lies about me, but what I don't do is DEMAND that person has to treat me better. That's stupid because I DON'T RUN THE UNIVERSE!! And that means I don't control other people.

That's like walking outside on a sunny day and raising my hands up in the air and screaming, "I demand it start raining!!!!" You know what would show even more stupidity? Getting mad if it didn't start to rain!

But that's what we're doing when we demand control over other people and events. It's no different than demanding it rain on a sunny day. We have the same control over the weather as we do over other people and things. Sometimes we forget that we don't run the universe.

So what do I do when others treat me badly? I make a wish! (But I don't click my heels together three times like Dorothy in *The Wizard of Oz* though...at least not in public.) Instead of demanding they treat me better, I WISH, HOPE, and STRONGLY PREFER that they treat me better, but I

You don't run the Universe, I do. You don't get what you want just by demanding it.

don't get mad about it.

Getting mad doesn't change the situation but it sure ruins my day and hurts my body...so I don't get mad very often and I don't stay mad very long.

The Proof Test

One of the ways to tell if a belief is true or false is to give it the proof test. If a belief is true, there is usually proof for the belief. It's just about that simple. If there is no proof, the belief is probably false and causing problems for you.

Some of the things we tell ourselves are irrational and not true. Is it possible to know what someone is thinking about you? Is it possible to read someone's mind? The answer is a big, fat, greasy NO!

Anytime you think something like, "I know he's lying about me" or "I know that teacher hates me," you're thinking something that may be untrue. If you hear the teacher say, "I hate you and wish you'd move to Australia," that's a different story. Then you've got proof!

Can we prove other people SHOULD do what we want? Remember, I'm not asking, "Would we

LIKE it if others did as we wanted?" That would be true and easy to prove. The question is SHOULD others do what we want. Let's look for proof. Is there any proof that teachers, parents or friends SHOULD do what we want? The answer is a big, slimy, hairy, greasy NO!

So it is important to think, "Do I have any proof for that thought?" Why? Because nobody wants to tell themselves NONSENSE. And when you believe stuff without proof, you're probably believing nonsense. Hey, we get told lots of nonsense by other people without telling it to ourselves, right?

This practice exercise will help you get better at telling the difference between true and false thoughts.

True vs. False Beliefs

DIRECTIONS: Next to each statement write T if the belief is True and F if the belief is False.

_____1. I wish I could get better grades.

_____2. If I get a "C" on the math test, it means I'm stupid.

_____3. My parents never let me go anywhere.

_____4. I don't like some subjects as much as others but I can stand them anyway.

_____5. If I don't get asked to go to prom, I'll die.

_____6. If I go to school with this haircut, everyone will make fun of me.

_____7. I wish things were easier but they don't have to be.

_____8. I'd like it if my parents would let me stay out later.

_____9. If my friends get mad at me, I don't have to think I'm a loser.

_____10. If I didn't get on the honor role I couldn't show my face at home.

_____11. Even if I look like a fool it doesn't mean I am a fool.

_____12. People ought to treat me with the respect I deserve.

Making the Change

Now that you've had some practice telling the difference between true and false thoughts, it is time to take one more step. This next exercise will give you practice changing demands into preferences...in a nut shell, this is what it is all about.

Once you know how to *consistently* 1) hear what you think to yourself, 2) tell the difference between true and false beliefs, and 3) change your false ideas to true thoughts, you're well on your way to overcoming your anger problem. Give this a try.

Changing the Irrational

DIRECTIONS: Underneath each irrational statement write a new, rational belief.

1. If my friends didn't like my new clothes it would mean I'm a complete loser.

____

____

____

2. I need to have things go easily or I can't take it.

3. He doesn't have the right to say that to me.

4. You have to agree with my idea because it's the best way to do it.

5. Things never go my way.

6. People shouldn't try to tell me what to do.

____

____

____

7. All teachers are idiots.

____

____

____

The Connection Between Stress & Anger

Some of you may be trying to figure out the connection between stress and anger. Just how do they relate?

Good question. I'll try to provide a good answer.

But first let me ask you a question. When are the times when you are most likely to lose your temper? What types of things are going on in your life?

1.______________________________________

____

2.______________________________________

____

3.______________________________________

____

Let me take a guess and see if you are anything like me. The times when I'm most likely to become angry usually involve these types of situations:

1. When I'm feeling sick.
2. When I'm working with or around people I just don't get along with.
3. When I'm tired.
4. When I've got many things to do and not enough time to do them.

You know what all of these things have in common? They are all **times when I'm under a lot of stress.** Now look back at your list of times when you are likely to lose your cool and see how many are times when you are under stress. That's the connection between stress and anger. **People are much more likely to experience problems with anger when they are under stress.**

So what do we do about that? Eliminate stress? That's not possible. Like I said earlier, the only people leading stress free lives are dead people and being dead pretty much ruins your chances of:

1) learning to ride a skateboard

2) becoming the world's greatest drummer
3) lots of other cool stuff

So if we can't eliminate stress, what can we do? To start with, you can make yourself aware that **when you are under a lot of stress, you are more likely to have problems with anger.** That way you can try to avoid certain people you don't get along with. You could try extra hard not to create a problem for your teachers because you'll know that you might explode and get into even more trouble.

Another thing to do is practice reducing your stress. Below write down four things you like to do when you feel stressed out.

1.____

____

2.____

____

3.____

____

4. ____

____

If you can't think of four things to reduce stress consider yourself lucky to be reading this book. Why? You may be learning things that will lengthen your life. I learned very few things in a math class that will help me live longer!

The facts are that anger and stress kills people. Everyday, all over the world, people are dying from the effects of anger and stress. Two of the leading causes of death in America are 1) heart disease and 2) strokes. Both are often associated with high stress and anger. The American Heart Association reported that people who have difficulties with their temper and have a tendency to explode during arguments **double** their risk of heart attacks.

I know the idea of reading about experiments is about as thrilling as watching your fingernails grow so I promise I'm only going to tell you about two of these scientific thing-a-ma-jigs. But please, pay close attention because what these scientists found is really important...it could lengthen your life.

The first experiment was on 1800 Western Electric workers who were given a test to measure feelings of anger. The workers were first asked to take this anger test in the late 1950's, way back when wearing grease in your hair was considered "cool." The workers were then watched to determine if higher scores in anger would predict health problems. **The workers who were more angry were one-and-a-half times more likely to develop heart disease and had a higher rate of cancer.**

The second experiment followed 255 medical students at the University of North Carolina and began, once again, in the late 1950's. The scientists doing this study contacted the students 25 years later and found that people with higher anger scores were **four to five times more likely to develop heart disease and seven times more likely to be dead.**

So even if you're not getting in trouble at school and even if you're not having lots of difficulties because of your anger, your body may still be suffering.

Learning to manage your stress will help you manage your anger. Below is a listing of things you might want to try when you're feeling stressed out.

Plan Ahead

Sometimes stress is unavoidable. For example, taking a driving test to get your license is something that is stressful, but unavoidable unless you plan on walking everywhere for the rest of your life. But sometimes we set ourselves up to be stressed out just because we haven't planned ahead.

For example, you've got a math test on Friday morning and you also promised to help some friends decorate the gym on Thursday night. Now you've got a difficult situation. You run the risk of either 1) not studying for the test and bombing it or 2) not following through on your promise to help and having your friends upset with you. If you would have planned ahead you could have either studied for the test a few nights earlier or asked your friends to do the decorating right after school.

There's a poster that says, "A lack of planning on your part does not create an emergency on my part." So true. A little planning can go a long way toward eliminating headaches down the road.

It's a good idea to always be looking ahead by at

least a week. It's probably best to plan ahead at least two weeks or a month to avoid time crunches. That way you've got enough time to try and changes things around when your life gets too crazy.

Call a Friend

When you're feeling stressed out it usually helps to talk to someone. Sometimes just talking to a friend or family member really helps. It's especially helpful if the person you're talking to has had the same kind of hassles in his or her life.

Keep in mind it would not be a good idea to call a friend and talk for two hours if your problem involves a lack of time! That might make the problem even worse. Tell your friend you can only talk for a few minutes and then stick to your plan.

Exercise

This is my all-time favorite stress buster. When I'm feeling really irritated and edgy, there's nothing I'd rather do than exercise. I always feel better after working out.

Any exercise is good and there certainly are a

lot to choose from. Lifting weights, aerobics, riding bikes, and a good old fashioned walk can re-energize you. Exercising will help you think more clearly, sleep better, and feel great throughout the day. It's the best way to literally burn off stress.

Your body will feel the effects of a workout after only twenty minutes. The time you spend exercising will actually save you time later because you'll be more productive after your workout.

Listen to Music

Relaxing with some tunes is a great way to unwind after a stressful day. Music takes your mind to a different place and helps you forget what you're mad about. I like to listen to different types of music depending on my mood and you're probably the same way. By the way, for those of you wondering, I'm writing this book with Led Zeppelin cranked in my headphones.

Do Something Artistic

Some people deal with stress by being creative. They take all the energy wound up in them and put it to good use by drawing, painting, or writing. Not only is art fun, it's a great stress reliever as well.

I can hear some of you already saying, "But I'm no good at drawing." So what! Neither am I but we're not talking about doing a piece of art that's going to hang in a museum someday. Try doodling. Remember that this art work is all yours and doesn't even have to be shown to other people. It's just to relax and have fun.

Take a Nap

Sometimes stress is made worse by being tired. We all get edgy and irritable when we're tired. If that's the case, catching a nap can help. There's increasing evidence that a majority of teenagers are walking around sleep deprived. We walk around yawning all day and then wonder why we're stressed out.

Meditate

Meditation is a great energizer. Not only does it relieve stress, it increases energy throughout the day.

Find a quiet place that has a comfortable chair. Shut your eyes and pay attention to your breathing. Try to slow down your breathing. Focus on your breathing and try to empty your mind. When thoughts do come in (and they will) just ignore them and go back to your breathing. It might be helpful to focus on one word. Think the word "one" as you breath as a means of keeping other thoughts out.

Start by trying to meditate for ten minutes at a time. You'll be surprised how much better you'll feel after just ten minutes. It's like a two hour nap!

Play a Musical Instrument

Another one of my favorite stress busters is playing a musical instrument of some kind. When I'm really uptight I try to let the energy inside me go right down my arms and out through my guitar. If I'm angry, I'll play some killer Metallica riffs. If I'm sort of sad, I play the blues. I always feel better when I'm done.

If you don't play a musical instrument, pick one up! It's never too late. If you've tried before, but weren't successful, maybe it's time to try again. I tried to learn the drums in 3rd grade and hated it. I picked up the guitar a few years later and absolutely loved it. Maybe you need to try a different instrument?

Read a Book

I get bummed out when I realize that very few middle school and high school students read for the fun of it. I also know the reason why. Two words...book reports! Those silly things can put people off reading for life. That's a shame because getting lost in a good book can be a blast.

I'd encourage you to try to read something funny or on a topic you're interested in like sports but whatever you read, just read! Some very smart person (I think it was Mark Twain) once said, "A person who does not read great literature has no advantage over a person who cannot read great literature." You go, Mark (or whoever said that). You rule, Twain dude!

Take a Bath

There's something very soothing about submerging in a hot bath. Unfortunately it's something we hardly ever do anymore because we feel like we can't take an extra ten minutes. Most of us take showers because they're faster. Take time to run a hot bath and soak until you're wrinkled.

Do Something Nice for Yourself

Everyone could use a little special treatment once in awhile. Somehow we get the message that it's wrong to take care of ourselves. It should be work, work, and more work until we drop over from exhaustion. Wrong!

Give yourself permission to do something a little extra nice. Go ahead, you deserve it. Now, I can't tell you what that is, but I know you can. What's something you can do that doesn't cost a lot of money and will be fun? A trip to the movies? A new haircut? That's for you to decide.

Imagine You Are Somewhere Special

Close your eyes and imagine you are in your favorite place. Maybe it's at the beach or your cousin's house. Mentally construct that place right now. Hear all the sounds. Picture those surroundings. Make it come alive in your imagination. You can take an imagination trip to make your day a little better. It's not the same as actually going there but it is a lot cheaper.

Draw your favorite place in the daydreamer's imagination above.

If you take the time to do some of the things listed above you'll experience a more peaceful life and have fewer conflicts with people because you'll be more relaxed. As stated earlier, you just may live longer too!

Errors in Thinking Leading to Increased Stress and Anger

People around the world are very different. We have slightly different colored skin, dress different, talk different and even eat different. There is one thing we all have in common...we all make mistakes!

We drop things, we drool on ourselves when we sleep (come on, admit it!), we spell words incorrectly, and, in general, we mess up a lot of stuff. As the chapter title tells you, we also make errors in the way we think and those mistakes increase our levels of stress and anger.

These errors in thinking occur in almost everyone from time to time...you, me, your teacher, and even your parents. The reason we make these mistakes has to do with the way our brain works.

Our brain does something that gets us into trouble...it takes shortcuts. Now don't get me wrong, shortcuts can be great but they can also backfire and the "shortcut" ends up being the "longcut." Let's go over a few of the ways we make errors in thinking and I think you'll understand.

Demonization

This error comes about from our tendency to make "demons" out of people we don't like or don't get along with. We mistakenly think that because people have one or two negative qualities they must be "all bad."

When we get to know people we almost always find they have some positive qualities, too. I'll be willing to bet this has happened to you. Describe a time in which you thought someone was "all bad," or a "demon" and how you learned that person was okay.

____

____

____

____

Our brain jumps from, "He did a bad thing" to "He's all bad." See, that's how the shortcut messes us up. Try to remember that even people who seem all bad have some good qualities, too.

Jumping to Conclusions

We have a tendency to act as if we know all the information when we really don't. That causes us to jump to conclusions.

What's the problem with jumping to conclusions? A lot of times our conclusions are WRONG! If you don't know all the information, how can you be certain you are correct. The answer is, "You can't."

If you can remember a time you've "jumped to conclusions" write it down below.

____

____

____

____

All or Nothing Thinking

This means that people think in extremes. People suffering from "all or nothing thinking" (also known as "black and white thinking") make a lot of mental predictions that are often wrong.

For example, you might think, "My friends

always do this to me. They **never** invite me to their parties." The result of that type of all or nothing thinking would be a lot of unnecessary anger and stress.

Ask yourself, "Is it true they **always** do this to me? That would mean I've **never, ever** been invited to a party. Is that true?"

My guess is that's not the truth, but when you tell yourself that ("They **never...**"), you feel as if it were reality and you get really, really mad.

Try this little experiment...pay attention to the times the words **always** and **never** leave your mouth and then try to determine if those statements are true. Once again, I doubt they will be which means you're creating a lot of anger and stress for yourself.

If you can remember a time you used "all or nothing thinking" write it down below.

____

____

____

____

"It Isn't Fair..."

A lot of people make themselves angry and stressed when they come across a situation they believe is not fair. They believe that **"Life has to be fair."** Where exactly is that written in stone anyway?

First off, nothing **has** to be fair just because you want it to be. It's okay to want it to be fair because there would be a lot of advantages if life were fair. But life isn't fair and I think it's safe to assume it will be at least partially unfair for the next few years. That's not a tragedy, just a reality. Most people manage to keep on having a pretty good time in life even though it's not completely, 100% fair.

Secondly, who gets to decide what is fair? Don't you think we'd have a lot of different ideas on what is fair?

Lastly, fair for whom? Let's say you believe it's fair for your parents to let you stay out until 11:00 p.m. on weekend night and they believe 10:30 p.m. is fair. Who's right? I don't know and nobody else does either. There is no absolutely right answer to the question, "What's fair?" It always depends.

Mind Reading

This occurs when we believe we **know** what's going on in people's minds. We think we know people so well that we know why they did what they did.

For example, a friend tells you he can't come over to your house Friday to watch videos and you assume this means he doesn't like you. Your brains says, "If he was my friend, he'd come over." Think about it, there might be a dozen reasons he can't make it. Maybe he's grounded Friday or he's going out of town or he's already told someone he'd go to the football game.

You can get all worked up thinking you know the reason why someone said or did something, but the truth is, you can't know unless the person tells you. And keep in mind that person could always tell you something that wasn't true! So let's leave mind reading to the silly people that pay $3.00 a minute on the "Psychic's Adventures Hotline" stuff.

I hope you are starting to see how we create a lot of headaches for ourselves as a result of these errors in thinking. You've taken an important first step by learning how we make errors in thinking, but there is more that needs to be done. The second step is paying attention to your thinking so you can pick out your errors **before** you act on them.

Okay, you folks with the psychic ability (just kidding), describe a time you've made the mistake of thinking you could read someone's mind.

____

____

____

____

Okay, now it is time to put it all together. Here is your chance to exercise those parts of your brain you haven't even used yet. Try this practice sheet. First, you will be asked to discover what you were thinking to make yourself angry. Next you'll try to change that thought to something that is not a demand. Feel free to return back to earlier chapters to review if you need some help. Good luck!

Anger Incident Practice Sheet

Directions: Complete the practice sheet with as much accuracy as possible. Pretend you are recording this event as if you were a video camera with sound. A video camera couldn't show someone being mean to you. It could show someone calling you names.

1. When did you make yourself angry?
   (What date and time was it?)

2. Where were you when you made yourself angry?

3. Who else was present?

4. As specifically as possible, describe what happened.

5. What did you say to yourself to make yourself angry? (Hint - Listen to your thoughts and see if you can hear any SHOULDS, MUSTS, or OUGHT TO BE'S)

6. How could you change what you said to yourself to change your feelings? (Hint - Try changing your demanding SHOULDS, etc. to preferences like I WISH...,IT WOULD BE NICE.....I'D LIKE.)

More Anger and Stress Management Skills

So far, so good. I hope you've been thinking about some of the ideas related to anger and stress management in this book. If you haven't, I'd like to say, "Just what the heck are you waiting for? A personal invitation? Well then, consider yourself invited!"

I wanted to tell you about a few other ideas you might find helpful. Keep in mind two words when reading these ideas..."lunch line." Think of these suggestions the way you view food in your lunch line. Some food look great and you can't wait to munch, but there's usually some spinach, too. The cool thing is that everyone who reads this book will identify different ideas as either pizza or spinach. You're free to choose.

Get a Pet

Caring for an animal can be a very rewarding experience. They can give you unending devotion and really don't ask that much of you. Just some

food, water, and a little love.

I think it's important to get a pet that you can spend time handling like a dog or cat. I'm not trying to disrespect turtles and pet snakes, but my narrow mind just can't understand how you can spend some quality time snuggling your boa constrictor! To each his or her own, I guess.

Here's the cool part...there is very solid evidence that people who own pets have better physical and emotional well-being when compared to people who don't own pets. Some studies show that being in the presence of certain animals (like a dog) can actually slow your heart rate and decrease your blood pressure.

Let's not forget the best part about having a pet. When everyone in the world is mad at you or thinks you're a dork, your pet will still be your buddy...and that's very cool.

STOP!

One simple and effective way of managing anger involves a thought stopping technique. Before I explain this technique, you need to start paying attention to your bodily "cues" that you're getting angry.

There are certain things that happen in your body right before you get mad. Some of you may not be aware when these "body cues" are happening, but it's important that you learn to recognize them. These cues are like a siren warning you just before you go ballistic. By recognizing what happens to your body before you get angry, you'll have a second to chill out before you do something really stupid or say something you'll regret later.

Everybody has some kind of body cue that occurs just before they get angry. Here are a few I've heard over the years. People say they:

- feel warm all over
- make fists with their hands
- have a clenched jaw and hold their teeth very tight

- start shaking all over
- feel their hearts begin to race

Like I said, everybody has a different set of body cues. Think for a moment and then write down what happens in your body just before you get angry.

1.____

2.____

3.____

Now, without looking up, why is it important to know your body cues?

____

____

____

In case you need some help, let's review once more. Knowing how your body feels just before you get angry is important because it will allow you a few seconds to think before you get angry and react. Acting *without* thinking usually leads to bad results.

Some of you may be thinking, "So even if I can recognize what I feel right before I get angry, so what? How is that going to help me? I'll still get mad." Not necessarily.

Here's where the STOP! technique can be used. When you become aware that you are getting angry (by paying attention to you body cues), you can cut off this anger by saying (or thinking) STOP! The reason I have both "say" or "think" STOP is that there are some places you can't yell out STOP. For example, during the middle of an exam would not be a good time to scream out the word STOP. That would be a good time to think the word STOP very forcefully. I know this sounds simple, but it really does work.

If you don't like that one, here's another one for you to try that is sort of based on the same idea of interrupting your thoughts. It's called the Distraction Technique.

Distraction Technique

This seems too simple to work but it does. You just think of something other than the situation you're getting ticked off about. But you know what happens? When you're getting mad, the ONLY thing you seem to be able to think about is the person or situation that's bugging you. It's sort of like when you're starving, pizza is the only thing on your mind.

That's why you need to decide what to think about BEFORE you start getting angry. This memory should be either the happiest or funniest thing you can remember. For example:

-The time you hit a home run to win a game.

-The time you got a great present for Christmas.

-Your best birthday party ever.

-The time you had an unexpected day off from school because of snow and ice.

I use a scene from way back when I was in 5th grade at my friend Kirk's house. Somebody said something funny and chocolate milk came blasting out of Kirk's nose! The milk came gushing out in two streams, one from each nostril. His eyes were as big as saucers because if you've ever had milk come out of your nose, it hurts a lot! Even today, many years later, when I distract myself from something that's going on that I don't like, there is no way I can be angry when I think about that scene.

Take a few minutes and think about your distraction scene then write it down below.

____

____

____

____

____

Make certain you've picked a good scene because it is important. Now you need to practice imagining this scene several times daily for the next few days. When you're sitting on the bus or waiting in line to eat lunch just close your eyes and picture your scene as clearly as you can. Bring in all the details that you can possibly remember.

What were the people wearing?
What were the sounds around you?
Were there any smells in the air?
Try to make the scene in your mind just like watching a video.

The idea is to switch to this distraction scene when you find yourself getting angry. Instead of thinking your parents are acting like jerks, concentrate on your scene. Instead of getting mad because someone borrowed a dollar and forgot to pay you back, concentrate on your scene until the feelings start to subside. Whenever you feel yourself getting angry, switch to your scene.

There's no way you can think of your distraction scene and still become angry. It is absolutely impossible. Since anger is produced by thinking demanding thoughts, thinking about a funny or happy memory will keep you from getting really upset. It will buy you time to chill out and that few seconds could be the difference between handling a situation and blowing it.

Right now, think back to a situation some time in the past where you got very angry. Recreate that scene in your mind and feel angry about it just like you did when it happened. Once you're feeling mad, switch to your new distraction scene and focus on it like a laser. Keep focusing on your distraction scene.

What happened to your anger? If you're really focusing on your distraction scene you anger will be either greatly diminished or gone.

Rational-Emotive Imagery or "the make believe game"

Lots of folks have one or two situations where they always seem to blow it...they always lose their cool at the same stuff. If that's you, I have something fun for you to try. This is my very best trick so use it with care. If this power were to fall into the wrong hands, there's no telling what evil adults could do with it!

The technique is called rational-emotive imagery and it is fairly easy to do. Imagine a situation you get mad about on a regular basis...it could be with a certain friend or it could be with a teacher.

Here's what you do...close your eyes and imagine the scene very clearly. Pretend you are actually there in your mind. See all the things going on in that situation. Hear the sounds that would be around you and everything about the situation. Make the scene real.

Next, go ahead and let yourself get good and ticked off just like you would if it were real life. Let yourself feel angry for several seconds.

Now, instead of being really, really mad...calm yourself down. Stay in that scene in your mind but keep working until you get yourself calmed down. When you get to the point where you've gotten your temper under control, take a deep breath and open up your eyes. Below, write down exactly what you thought to yourself to calm yourself down.

____

____

____

If you were able to calm yourself down, chances are you have just written down a rational or true belief. Look at the belief you just wrote down and ask yourself:

1) Can I prove the belief to be true? yes no
2) Is the belief most likely to bring about positive results? yes no
3) Is the belief likely to get me into or out of trouble? into trouble out of trouble

Once you've determined the belief is a true/rational belief, **repeat** the same practice exercise **everyday** and **several times a day** if you can. Practice thinking the true/rational belief you've just recorded when you are trying to calm yourself down. Write it down on a small card and carry it with you for times when you feel yourself beginning to get angry. You can use your distraction scene until you are calmer. Then practice this new, rational thought.

I know, I know...it sounds too simple to work but it does.

I know, I know...it sounds boring. Maybe. But would you rather have more time now or more hassles because of your anger?

Find Something Funny in the Situation

Most situations have something funny in them. You just have to look for it.

If you don't believe me try this little experiment. Think of a something you used to be angry about that you *now* think is hilarious. Haven't you ever had a situation that didn't seem funny at the time, but later you laughed yourself silly thinking about it? Almost everybody can think of something like that.

A few months ago I came in from our backyard and didn't realize I had dog do-do on my shoe. When my wife pointed it out to me I was really mad because 1) we don't have a dog so it must have been one of the neighbor's dogs and 2) I was walking on our new carpet at the time. So I started hopping around on one foot getting all mad and stuff. My wife started laughing at me because I was hopping around like an idiot. I didn't think that was too funny then but we laugh our heads off about it now.

Here's the important part...if something that happened is funny now it must have been funny then. Whatever situation you're mad about has stayed exactly the same. *The only thing that has changed is how you think about it now.* I still had dog poop on my shoe while I was hopping around the living room. I think it's funny now because I've stopped thinking it was such a big deal. Try to keep that in mind when you're getting all stressed out about something. Maybe there is something really funny and you're just not seeing it.

Time Projection

One last one before we move on...this one involves mentally putting yourself into the future. Here's how it works.

When you getting all stressed out and mad about something, ask yourself a question. *Is this situation going to be a major hassle in my life five years from now?* Chances are the answer will be, "No." If it's not something that is going to be bugging you five years in the future then it probably is something you can handle now *without* getting all stressed out. In other words, you're probably getting more worked up than you need to be.

See if you can think of a situation from five years ago that is still affecting your life today. If you can, try comparing the situation you're currently stressed about to the one from five years ago. Is this problem as serious as the previous situation? If it is, do everything you possible can to prepare for it. If it's not, relax and realize the problem will be nothing but a memory in a short period of time.

Now it's time to measure how much you've changed since the start of this book. Once again, complete the anger survey below as honestly as possible. There are no wrong answers. Circle the number which best reflects how strongly you agree or disagree with each statement. When you've finished, compare this score with your score earlier in the book.

The Anger Survey

Strongly Disagree					Strongly Agree

1. I get angry when things don't go as planned.

1	2	3	4	5	6

2. Other people make me angry.

1	2	3	4	5	6

3. Life should be fair.

1	2	3	4	5	6

Strongly Disagree					Strongly Agree

4. When I don't do well, I get very angry with myself.

   1 2 3 4 5 6

5. Things have to be my way or I get angry.

   1 2 3 4 5 6

6. The world has to be a better place to live.

   1 2 3 4 5 6

7. My family can <u>make</u> me get angry.

   1 2 3 4 5 6

8. There are a lot of things that ought to be better than they are right now.

   1 2 3 4 5 6

9. I can't control my temper.

   1 2 3 4 5 6

10. I get mad when people don't act like
I think they should.

1 2 3 4 5 6

TOTAL ______________

TOTAL from earlier in the book _________

If you're less angry and thinking less demanding thoughts, your score will go DOWN. If you've actually done worse with your anger, your score will go UP.

Decreased by ____ Say, "I'm doing better!"
Increased by ____ Say, "I need to work harder!"

Summary

I've done these exercises with hundreds of students over the years and I can predict where most of you will be at the end of the book.

1) **Some of you will have made great progress.**

You will already be well on your way to controlling your anger instead of letting your anger and stress control you. You've worked hard at the lessons and really PRACTICED. Other people and things have an impact, but don't control how you feel anymore.

2) **Some of you will be making progress but still struggling.**

You'll understand that you cause yourself to be angry and stressed out, but haven't learned how to keep yourself from getting ticked off. You can talk the talk, but not walk the walk. You understand it, but can't live it yet.

That's okay. Learning these skills is not easy. You've had a habit of getting angry and stressed out for a long time and it takes hard work to overcome this tendency. Focus on the **Distraction** technique, explained in an earlier chapter, until you become better at arguing yourself out of your anger.

3) **Some will feel it is hopeless.**

You might even believe there is no way to ever overcome your problems. NOT TRUE. It just takes more work. Think about it this way for a minute.

Whenever you're learning something new, there is a period of time when you can't do it and the new skill seems hopeless. There was a time when you couldn't tie your own shoes! You couldn't tell time! You couldn't go to the bathroom by yourself! By now you've all mastered these everyday tasks. So don't give up.

Thanks for taking the time and energy to read this book. I sincerely hope you've learned something worthwhile. Managing the thoughts that cause your anger and stress will become a habit with enough practice. Once you learn to control yourself rather than having others control you, the sky is the limit.

Discounts on Ordering Additional Copies of the "Hot Stuff" Books

Additional copies of the "Hot Stuff" books can be order by contacting:

LGR Publishing
3219 N.W. C St.
Richmond, IN 47374
(800) 369 - 5611
(765) 939 - 8924 (fax)
mcphd@infocom.com (email)

The discount schedule for bulk orders is:

10 - 25 copies	25% discount from $9.95
26 - 100 copies	50% discount from $9.95
101 and above	55% discount from $9.95